# Talking About the Past

Nick Hunter

Heinemann LIBRARY

Chicago, Illinois

© 2015 Heinemann Library
an imprint of Capstone Global Library, LLC
Chicago, Illinois

Edited by Catherine Veitch and Gina Kammer
Designed by Steve Mead and Peggie Carley
Picture research by Mica Brancic
Production by Helen McCreath
Originated by Capstone Global Library Ltd

**Library of Congress Cataloging-in-Publication Data**
Cataloging-in-publication information is on file with the Library of Congress.
ISBN 978-1-4846-0232-4 (hardcover)
ISBN 978-1-4846-0236-2 (paperback)
ISBN 978-1-4846-0244-7 (eBook PDF)

**Acknowledgments**
Alamy: Classic Stock, 7, OJO Images Ltd/Paul Bradbury, 5; AP Images:
Manuel Balce Ceneta, 9; Getty Images: Archive Photos/Lawrence Thornton,
21, Blend Images/Tanya Constantine, 25, Camille Tokerud, cover, Cultura/
Monty Rakusen, 26, Hulton Archive/Bert Hardy, 20, Hulton Archive/
Imagno, 19, Hulton Archive/Three Lions, 16, The Image Bank/Jupiterimages,
8, Popperfoto, 14, 24, Retrofile/George Marks, 13, Retrofile/H. Armstong
Roberts, 4; iStock: Hulton Archive, 15, Mark Bowden, 6; Newscom: ZUMA
Press/Ana Venegas, 28; Shutterstock: Andrzej Sowa, 29, Elzbieta Sekowska,
12, Michael Jung, 17, oliveromg, 23; SuperStock: age fotostock/Ulysses, 27,
ClassicStock.com, 10, 18, 22, imagebroker.net, 11

Every effort has been made to contact copyright holders of material
reproduced in this book. Any omissions will be rectified in subsequent
printings if notice is given to the publisher.

All the Internet addresses (URLs) given in this book were valid at the time
of going to press. However, due to the dynamic nature of the Internet, some
addresses may have changed, or sites may have changed or ceased to exist
since publication. While the author and publisher regret any inconvenience
this may cause readers, no responsibility for any such changes can be accepted
by either the author or the publisher.

# Contents

Some words are shown in bold, **like this**.
You can find out what they mean by looking
in the glossary.

# Living History

We learn history to find out what happened in the past. That can mean learning about people who lived a long time ago. History can also be about things that happened just a few years ago.

▲ Your grandparents played with different toys than the ones you have now.

Sometimes you find out about history from books, TV, or the **Internet**. You can also find out about history by talking to people about their lives.

▲ People who are older than you can tell you true stories about the past.

# Changing Times

You can learn about the past from older people such as your parents and teachers. They will tell you that things have changed during their lives. Listening to people's memories can be amazing.

▲ Who are the people you know who could tell you about the past?

People's memories can help you find out about your family, your town, or events in the past. Try to talk to different people who you know. Each person will remember slightly different things.

▲ What did your grandparents watch on TV when they were younger?

# Asking Questions

You can ask questions about the past in an **interview**. You could interview someone you know, such as a grandparent. Your school could invite someone to talk about an event or time you are studying in class.

▲ Interview tips: Find a quiet place and make sure everyone can hear. Ask the person's permission if you want to record the interview.

Make sure you know what your interview will be about so you can plan what questions to ask. The best questions have lots of possible answers, such as "What was school like when you were a child?"

▲ Ask your questions one at a time and listen carefully to the answers.

# Getting Around

You could ask about how the way we travel has changed. When your grandparents were young, there were fewer cars and they looked very different.

▲ Today there are around 20 times more cars on the world's roads than in 1950.

Steam trains were powered by burning coal. They were noisy and dirty but many people still work to **restore** them. Maybe one of your grandparents could tell you about traveling by steam train.

▲ Steam trains were still widely used 60 years ago. Today's trains are powered by electricity or other fuel.

# Food in the Past

You will see foods from around the world in your local supermarket. Find out what people ate when your parents and grandparents were young. Were their favorite foods the same as yours?

▲ Ask your parents or grandparents to help you make the foods they liked best as children.

**Modern** kitchens are packed with **gadgets** such as microwave ovens and dishwashers. Fifty years ago, these gadgets were unusual. Find out what other new gadgets were missing from homes in the past.

▲ Find out what people used instead of microwave ovens and other kitchen appliances.

# Changing Fashion

Clothes change because people like to wear different **fashions**. Some of our clothes today are made from new light and comfortable materials. Many of these materials had not been invented when your grandparents were children.

◀ Your relatives may even have kept some of the clothes they used to wear.

In the 1940s, children's clothes were similar to the ones their parents wore. Older people will be able to tell you about the clothes they used to wear.

▲ Do you think these children's clothes were more comfortable than the clothes you wear?

# Going to School

Schools have always taught children to read, write, and do math. But the equipment that teachers use has changed. When your parents were at school, there were few computers or whiteboards.

▲ Does this classroom from 1950 look like yours? What are the differences?

You could ask your teachers to talk to you about what school was like when they were young. What did they learn and which books did they read? What did they like and dislike about school?

Find out which books your teacher enjoyed as a child.

# Having Fun

Most people can remember the toys they played with when they were young. Some old toys were similar to modern ones. In the past, they were made of wood or metal rather than **plastic**.

▲ Computer games became popular in the 1970s. They were very different from the games you play now.

Your grandparents may have played the same sports as you, but the equipment and clothing looked quite different. Try talking to a coach from a local sports club to tell you how things have changed.

▲ Leather soccer balls were heavier and harder to kick than modern plastic ones.

# Shopping and Working

Before there were big supermarkets, people went shopping at small stores. **Grocers** sold fruit, vegetables, and other goods. Shops were usually in the center of towns.

▲ In shops like this grocer's, customers had to ask the shopkeeper for what they wanted to buy.

Many people who worked in offices used typewriters to **type** letters and other **documents**. Today office workers have computers. Ask people who have **retired** about the work they used to do.

▲ Students at this school learned to type quickly in the 1940s.

# Happy Holidays

Fifty years ago, traveling **abroad** on vacations was unusual. Families often took trips close to where they lived. Ask people about their first memories of going on vacations.

▲ Campers became popular for vacations as more people owned cars.

People remember how they celebrated holidays such as Christmas when they were young. They may have photographs to share. These photos will show how festivals were different.

▲ Families often keep photos of festivals and celebrations from the past.

# Good and Bad Times

Big events can change ordinary lives. World War II lasted from 1939 until 1945. It was a difficult time for many people. Do you know anyone who remembers the war?

▲ Many British children had to move to the country because the cities where they lived were bombed during the war.

Many people were not born in the country they live in now. Talk to people in your community about what life was like when they first moved to your country. How have things changed for them?

▲ Many cities are home to people who have moved from another country.

# Investigating History

Some people spend all their time learning about history. **Historians** from a local museum could show you things that were used in the past.

▲ These children are learning about knights and castles.

**Archaeologists** dig up evidence about the past from under the ground. They find remains of buildings or tools that are hundreds of years old. These things help them to figure out how people used to live.

▲ An archaeologist can tell amazing stories about life in the past.

# Your History Project

It is important to keep records of what you learn from talking to people. You could record your interview or use a pen and paper to take notes.

▲ If you record your interview, it will be easier to share it with others.

You can use what you learn from talking to people to create a history project. Include old photos and things that you have learned from other books. You could share what you have learned with your school.

▲ There are lots of other **sources** you can use to learn about the past.

# Find Out More

## Books

Williams, Brian. *Life in World War II*
  (Unlocking History). Chicago: Raintree, 2010

Woolf, Alex. *A Photographic View of Schools*
  (Past in Pictures). London: Wayland, 2014

## Websites

**http://www.americaslibrary.gov/jb/wwii/jb_wwii_
subj.html**
See a timeline and discover more about World War II.

**http://kids.usa.gov/history/index.shtml**
Watch videos, play games, and see original historical
documents on this website.

**sounds.bl.uk/Oral-history/Opie-collection-of-
children-s-games-and-songs-**
Listen to children's games and songs from the past
with this collection of recordings.

# Glossary

**abroad** in another country

**archaeologist** someone who digs in the ground to uncover remains from the past

**document** any piece of written or printed material

**fashion** style of clothing that is popular at a certain time

**gadget** electronic or other machine that does a useful task

**grocer** shop that sells general food and household goods

**historian** person whose job is to study history

**Internet** system of connected computers that we can use to send and receive information around the world

**interview** conversation in which one person is being asked lots of questions to get information

**modern** new or up-to-date

**plastic** type of material that is made from oil and can be molded into different shapes

**restore** to bring back to an original state

**retire** to stop working, usually because of a person's age

**source** thing that can be used to find out information about history, including photos, objects, books, and newspapers

**type** to write using a keyboard, such as on a computer or typewriter

# Index